EQUINOX
AND OTHER POEMS

EQUINOX
AND OTHER POEMS

BY
DAVID R. SLAVITT

LOUISIANA STATE UNIVERSITY PRESS
Baton Rouge and London 1989

Copyright © 1985, 1986, 1987, 1988, 1989 by David R. Slavitt
All rights reserved
Manufactured in the United States of America

97 96 95 94 93 92 91 90 89 88   5 4 3 2 1

Designer: Sylvia Malik Loftin
Typeface: Weiss
Typesetter: The Composing Room of Michigan, Inc.
Printer: Thomson-Shore, Inc
Binder: John H. Dekker & Sons, Inc.

Library of Congress Cataloging-in-Publication Data

Slavitt, David R., 1935–
  Equinox and other poems.

  I. Title.
PS3569.L3E67 1988   811'.54   88-8239
ISBN 0-8071-1484-7
ISBN 0-8071-1485-5 (pbk.)

The paper in this book meets the guidelines for permanence and durability of the Committee on Production Guidelines for Book Longevity of the Council on Library Resources. ∞

Some of the poems in this collection have appeared previously in the following periodicals: *Ontario Review, Southern Poetry Review, New Criterion, Negative Capability, Kansas Quarterly, Painted Bride Quarterly, West Branch, Four Quarters,* and *Georgia Review.*

The author is grateful to the Pennsylvania Council on the Arts for the Fellowship in Literature that was helpful in the preparation of this manuscript.

FOR JANET

CONTENTS

I
Canaletto's Ruin   3
Nevelson   5
Used Furniture   6
Refinement   7
Twins   8
The Field of Light   9
Mal des Fleurs   10
An Explanation of the Dolby System   12
Remarks   13
Performance   14
Cut Flowers   16
Forio   17
Pantoum   19
Consent   20
Matisse's Tablecloth   21

II
Circus Costumes   25
Henry Taylor Shows Me His Parents' Barn   28
Plodders   30
Lummox   31
Fizz   32
Sonnet   33
Rite for a Deceased Cat   34
Flea   36
Satisfaction   38
Snowfall   40
Letter to a Grandchild   41
Another Letter to a Grandchild   43
Solstice   46
Equinox   47   *powerful*

I

Canaletto's Ruin

Those clouds, stalled over what is left of the ruined
arch, are themselves another arch, their lines
a parallel that cannot be accidental.

Saplings growing, meanwhile, into the sky
from atop the masonry blur the hewn stone
to fluffiness. Canaletto's wit is at work,

as there in the human figures crossing the rickety
bridge or, below, in the boats on the dark water,
going about their business, diminutions

of the stone figures along the pavillion's roof
or of the heroic bust in the niche of the sunlit
wall, not yet abraded by time's roughness—

that shadow, nevertheless, almost too dramatic,
aslant at the base of the structure, is clear enough.
The day is nearly done, the sun about to

sizzle into the water—and yet the mood
is not melancholy, but rather say clear-eyed:
see the liveliness, there in the red tarboush

on the gondolier's head, or there in the loving
attention with which the wall's discoloring lichens
are executed. Such details redeem

or at least offer the comfort that nature's voracious
encroachments may be, for awhile anyway, postponed.
This is, after all, a painting. The sun will not

ever set; the crumbling building will not
further delapidate, nor will those human
figures progress even an inch in their

preoccupations. Ruin is what the painter
dares, defies, as he stretches his canvas taut
to assure us, even to catch us, panicky now

and almost ready to leap. That artifice cannot
last is what his painting says and then
unsays, which may be why we have an odd

vertiginous feeling, from contemplating a structure
not to be found on some backwater island
but in that shared dream (if not the nightmare)

Venice floats on like some improbable bubble
the lagoon has spat up that will at any instant
pop—and we wake to the realization of loss

of whatever we love most. That awesome wreck,
towering so as to dwarf the human figures,
is home, *signori, signore*, yours and mine,

if only we could steel ourselves to admit
so drastic a decline. Footfalls that echo
on those wide terazzo floors sound in the mind

above the plash of oars—or are they whispers
of blood in the eardrum's artery? Those halls
from which we are overthrown are dark, filthy,

and repellent now, but we stare at them, fascinated,
clenching in impotent rage the useless fists
we never even raised to try to prevent

the disgrace we now inhabit, this abject ruin
we contrive one way or another to live with. Closing
the eyes should help, but doesn't at all—the image

persists. Those figures only maintain a civil
and mutual pretense, their glances averted
from the huge pile that dominates their lives,

and at night, alone, each of them sees his own
vision of ruin, as vivid as any painting.
Who then would need to look up, to confirm

his worst fears? They know perfectly well
what's there, can hear the water slap at the stone,
and feel in their hearts something like that stolid

coolness of stone that may be our best hope.

NEVELSON

These bits and pieces of civilization, dowels,
barrel staves, newels, finials, the seats
of wooden chairs, ordered together and painted
matte black or flat white as her wit
and whim dictate, prompt us to imagine
pardon—not that our own dry bones will rise
so again, but it's pleasant to see survivors
by an act of will restored, improved, cherished.
What a wreck it must have been—we can guess,
extrapolating from our own disasters.
Her pieces float in state in a gallery air
of costliness, and the prices should be high
for the odds are long against such grace, such rescue,
such reconciliation of taste and love.

Used Furniture

They lug elderly sofas and tables in
and out, chests, credenzas, rocking chairs,
and nightstands into their stores and out again.

When the weather is fine, they leave some on display,
out on the sidewalk. You go to the liquor store
on Market Street and you can't miss them, poised

where the slums and student housing meet, which is right
and how those stores have lasted. Nearly worthless
the pieces of furniture move with a life of their own,

survivors of deaths, evictions, and even sometimes—
as when a number hits—good luck. They find
a comfortable level of hardship to hang out with,

shrug off or give in to. In their glare
we try not to let our apprehension show:
in that part of town it is provocation, even

invitation. Spirit's the thing, booze,
bought by the half gallon. Safe at home,
I'm jumpy but keep my feelings hidden. The lesson

still holds, for I know where some of these tables
have stood and the chairs have sat. Where will they go
from here? Don't ask! In the heart of the wood, stirring

as if in a breeze that once tousled boughs
of the living trees, predators' screams and their victims'
cries are barely stilled. A chair, a table

will turn on you, will suddenly turn vicious,
or, like some bitch in heat, take off one day
to mill with her own kind out there on the sidewalk,

comparing scars and daring the lives to come.

Refinement

Ours are plenty's penalties—gout, girth,
atherosclerosis, kidney stones,

and ennui. Below stairs, cook goes crazy
trying to dream up novelties, pleasing, teasing . . .

Our meals, social or business occasions, divide
morning from afternoon, evening from night.

They say much of the world gets up from the table
hungrier than we are, sitting down.

It's wit on the carte, under the salver's silver
cover. The maître wishes us bon appetit.

But haven't you heard? There's a new drink, a new
picture or poem, or way to read some old

picture or poem. What difference can it make
(and how long ago did you stop thinking it could)?

Meanwhile, the youngsters with appetites and energies
nothing less than alarming and woeful manners

gobble whatever's in reach, novelists, painters,
poets, composers, and often one another . . .

One turns queasy. Indeed, it may be said
that's what we teach—to sniff and make a face.

TWINS

Taste and appetite accommodate,
but barely, the one too ready with its *No, thank you,*
and the other's eager *Yes, please* always shining
on spittled lips.

Taste deigns to nibble while appetite gnaws
until, at the end, the yoke is lifted and each,
freed, flies off to its separate heaven
to grow to its perfection, or to dwindle.

Don't they miss how it was, the constant persuading,
seducing the sulky twin, overcoming reluctance,
each meal and morsel another bargain
and new balance? Not a bit: they thrive
king of the jungle, lord of the desert, each
supreme in fullness or emptiness, and both
killers, as we always knew they were.

The Field of Light

The road, past Worcester and sundown,
unwound in hollows' evergreen
shadows, velvet billows: the firm
earth melted under the wheels.
But then, at a turn onto high ground,
I entered onto a field of light.
Light was its crop, a yield of gold
that oozed up like the sweat of plums.

For five minutes the marvel held me
hushed with delight in its reprieve
until, at another turn, it passed
as inspiration often does,
leaving me with miles to go
and accelerating into grimness.

Mal des Fleurs

As we pass the construction site, we hesitate,
try not to let the purposive hammer blows
distract us with their unselfconscious arcs
of energy, but attend, rather, to random
sparks that willy-nilly arise and hark
at the rhythms of two workmen whose poundings only
rarely coincide. *Extase!* But they
resent such elevation, their honest labor
suddenly rarefied. We must show tact,
be sneaky even. Frivolousness ought never
insult the innocent objects of its interest,
even though at the last judgment we all
face arbitrariness at least as hard
as ours must seem to them. Well, let it come.
Bravura ought to be brave—we'll take our chances.

To carry this off requires a certain spunk
without which we surely drown in sentiment's
swamp where most men live, resembling logs
with snouts at the water level, greedy to chew
and digest whatever is other. See, one yawns,
and provides, by the way, a gorgeous display of odontic
crenellation he cannot comprehend
let alone have intended. Which then is the fiercer
predator, that simple beast or you
or I, stalking whatever is rare, whatever
catches our jaded attention (we're proud of that
and call ourselves refined)? Pounce! And we're likely
to gobble landscapes whole, not for survival
or even from honest appetite, but only
habit and talent, of course. Whatever we can
do, we feel we must. *Voir: savoir:
pouvoir*—the pitiless declension is
familiar and inexorable. And right.

A whistle blows and the workmen quit, but we,
still on duty, can never set our tools
down and disappear into some bar.
Fastidiousness will not, like honest grime,

wash off. We idle home, where even the plants
have abandoned nature, adapted themselves, become
artful and forced . . . which is why we care for them
so ardently. Delicate, yet they thrive
in our hothouse atmosphere and preen as no
outdoor specimen would, or not since Eden.

An Explanation of the Dolby System

What it does, we have done for years in our own
ears and heads, encoding and decoding,
undoing performances, restoring them to their notes
from which we perform, on which we work our own
will, attending as we please, or ignoring
whatever we will, whatever is displeasing,
surface noises, for instance, the hiss we'd hiss
if we supposed these mere machines could hear
or react to our reactions. They boost here
and then diminish there, to return to a state
better than real, if not truer than true.
What possibilities are there for engineers
to tantalize us with, what high-tech tricks?
Dolby meals? Dolby sex? What Dolby
days and nights can we spend, lolling on some
Dolby beach? Thus, must the dead dream
their lives' perfections, parodies, and yearn,
in a heaven where the slag-heaps are pure gold,
for incidental grit, for imperfections.

REMARKS

for Robert Pinsky

Over the years, he learned that by taking pains
he could avoid the obvious pitfalls
of thought, vision, of sensibility,
and of the language. One learns what is not
a poem. What is not not a poem,
may prove perhaps to be of worth.
But how can he be satisfied with glimpses,
with sojourns? Poems are not high-toned resorts.
One wants to live there, settle. Imagine how,
at a reading, those remarks between the poems,
in the words of explanation, the disarming
gestures we all make, the apology for
such impositions, demands for heightened attention,
whatever we say to take the curse off it,
to deflate the pretensions of poetry, imagine those
vampings in the same diction, with the same
elevated delivery . . . Who would know?

But a seamlessness between the poems
and what is not the poems? What an awesome
gift of spirit, vision, linguistic invention!
The sympathetic, small, but intelligent
audience, puzzled, captivated, rapt
can hardly breathe, can't tell when not to clap.

Performance

This is like that. A modest claim
a child could make, and did, and admiring
faces beamed brighter than suns
at their son's promise. This is like
the fall: an amateur turning pro,
and the eyes rove, searching further
occasions for praise, acquiring dirty
habits of seeing and saying. Performance
and the hankering after applause distort
vision and skew the mind. The world
dislikes such preening; the smart-assed kid
gets sent to his room, rebuffed to sulk
and suffer. There, looking out of a window,
he may find solace in how a branch
of the oak tree quivers after a squirrel
has made its leap—like the twitch of a nerve.
At it again? Now, however,
only for private comfort—another
compromise, another distraction
from the thing-in-itself. Even to glimpse it
requires reluctance, narrowed lids
and tight lips on which untruth's
unlovely taste lingers, a taint
one learns to loathe. Up in the sky
the only beaming now is from
a pale moon long ago
talked to death, but this is redeeming:
recognizing that there's no
gain, no advantage, still he feels
sometimes an impulse, even the need,
irresistible, to break
a decent silence and admit
something even better, that rare,
clarifying, satisfying,
significant similitude.
It cannot beguile his old losses
away, but the small satisfaction
one takes in seeing and seeing through

is like a new stamp on the visa
pages of his limp passport,
his *permis de séjour* extended
at least for awhile. A minor but vital
triumph, it perhaps deserves
a cognac with his evening coffee.

Cut Flowers

Beyond the money and the continual
calculation you hate (and after awhile
abandon, resigning yourself to being cheated),
beyond the perils of traffic coming at you,
and the odd billboards with meaningless signs
indicting your denseness, there is the constant risk
of getting lost—that the streets at any moment
may diverge from the plan, reorient, depart
from sense itself. How can a cityscape
just gulp its landmarks down? But they are gone,
and the long row of sooty buildings is dark,
menacing, and there is no escape. Your dreams
will return you here, on an Inward Bound test
(can you survive on a huge handful of coins
that are not enough for a phone call or even the toilet?).
There is no one to turn to, nobody you can trust,
for the faces are all unreadably blank (again,
your fault). You cannot even rely
on your own emotions—jet lag having turned you
jumpy, apt to drowse off at the theater
or to sit up full awake in the small hours.
But then, one morning, the weather relents a little
and you pass a shop window and notice flowers,
all those bunches of flowers, ready to open,
red, red and white, pink and white, and all
going giddy, fainter, cut, and the fields
or hothouses they came from fading. Tears?
No, but later, the idea begins to take root.
And once that's happened, once you have made that happen,
you are no longer absolutely a stranger.

FORIO

German tourists now come for the mud,
the brownish water in pools from the hot springs,
their peculiar cheese-and-bologna breakfasts, and one
another. Auden, were he somehow to return,

would be distressed, but then distress would be
familiar and what the Mezzogiorno means,
what Ischia anyway meant. The people were mean,
poisoned one of his cats, and cheated him more

even than vague and preoccupied English poets
ought to expect. The island, nevertheless,
has pleasant wines and, at Forio, a prospect
of water one way and Mount Epomeo

looming the other (with buggery and sunshine
at bargain rates Inglesi delight in). What
more could a man want? He toddled down
the hill on his tender feet to inspect the monsters—

contorted heaps of lava the old volcano
had spat into the sea—to buy a paper,
and have a coffee or perhaps an aperitivo
before he trudged back. He wanted only

what most writers want—to be left alone,
but the children teased him, as even these poor
kids will, an odd enough duck. His "Basta!"
was the victory they'd get before they let him

go. That he could, leaving, bless the region
shows his generous nature, or perhaps his modest
expectations. The name of his street is changed,
and nobody here remembers an English poet.

Not even the workmen, affixing one end of the frame
for the colored lights they dearly love for the feast
of one of those "minim saints" to Auden's house,
know who lived inside. Still he has joined

his list of "sacred meridian names—Vico,
Verga, Pirandello, Bernini, Bellini,"
and those gods who arrange such matters have contrived
that the decorations attach to the proper building.

Pantoum

The lines repeat themselves like hammer blows,
always verging on nonsense, and end-stopped
as bad poetry is (and life, God knows).
A comfort when that second shoe has dropped . . .

Always verging on nonsense, and end-stopped,
a Malayan form, it had a vogue in France.
A comfort when that second shoe has dropped,
the *repeton*. It's like a clumsy dance.

A Malayan form, it had a vogue in France
where people toy with emotion. When griefs come,
the *repeton*. It's like a clumsy dance
one dances at words' failure, almost dumb.

Where people toy with emotion when griefs come,
with Hugo, Leconte de Lisle, and Baudelaire
one dances at words' failure, almost dumb,
moved, moving in the pantoum's heavy air.

How do we get through it? One need not say
what bad poetry is, and life. God knows!
Fooling around like this, we learn to pray,
and the lines repeat themselves like hammer blows.

Consent

With greater or lesser assurance, you come to ask
for the hand of my daughter,
with more or less poise . . .
It does not much matter.

I give my permission of course;
I do, but I wonder
what difference it makes, why you bother asking.
Are you so punctilious, or do you think I am?

Perhaps you will be happy together,
perhaps not. But you will never understand her as I do,
will not see in her queenly gestures poignant traces
of girlishness almost gone, even lovable awkwardness.

The manners of a sophisticated woman
are like the gloss of a finished poem;
what you admire defeats you, that glossy sheen blinds you
to her simplest impulse.

I, who have brought her to this remarkable conclusion,
can give her to you with hardly a pang
and even wish you well, knowing how much
I keep back for myself.

Matisse's Tablecloth

That the red and white stripes of a tablecloth
can organize a room, enlivening both
it and the beholding eye (its bands

of color and no-color, horizontal or
vertical, or jauntily aslant),
leading attention, training and constraining,

Matisse discovered, having striven for years
to see through to such simplicity.
Vision can focus to wisdom, and light can be

not merely an emblem but knowledge itself.
There it was, and had been all along,
domestic wildness, wild as wilderness

under the earthenware plates. Under his nose.
To stare at a thing as a child stares, to be
that child again, naughty enough to ask

the right fanciful questions—whether the cloth
is white with red stripes or the other way?
Or whether the red areas squeeze the white

which otherwise would spread, or fly apart—
or the other way around. There is energy surely,
a wild swirl of it, jumbling. See how those rows

are imposed, shimmering compromise. The paints
on the palette left to themselves revert to muck.
Caught in the fabric's weft they pace like tigers

in zoos. In the darkness, one might hear their snarls.
Who has not known with Matisse un-ease's nagging
(as the poor know the greed with which millionaires

began)? Who has not felt, in a strange city
walking the streets with an hour to kill, the need
for some small object, a trinket—a recognition

or answer in a shop window; a flag
by which to lay some claim to all that is foreign,
even the reflection of that almost

familiar face; or something to lug back,
something to touch? We open our purses and spend,
for at home it is more difficult, even desperate:

there we must be tourists, learn to remark
at surfaces of things, glints, dullnesses—
and risk losing our way a block from our door.

II

CIRCUS COSTUMES

1

I never knew my grandfather, my father's
father. A figment I had to invent him from
thin air or, harder, correct from the misleading
hints I'd got from the clinkers of love and rage
still warm in my father's heart's furnace.
Who approaches altars in the shrines
that families are without dread? Had he
lived, I might have seen him plain (grandchildren
can) without that shimmer of heated air
that rises so often between fathers and sons.

2

What do I know of my grandfather that I
trust, that I did not learn at secondhand
from my father? A picture, now lost, that I think
I remember; and my aunt's enlightenment
of why they moved to Bridgeport, why their plan
for a tailoring shop and gas station was not
totally crazy: the circus wintered there,
and my grandfather could make costumes for clowns,
acrobats, and bareback riders, silks
and satins, fancy suits with ruffs and spangles.

3

My father never mentioned this, preferred
the story of the atelier in Paris
where his father and uncle made the wedding dress
for Alexandra, a hundred women sewing
seed pearls on the train. Royalty! Class!
Or anyway not that louche other . . . The low
life, like alcohol or other minor
vices, must not be made too much of. Let
the children have their first sips in comfort,
at home, or else it becomes a mystery, looms.

4

Or rather say there was too much love, a hugging
that nearly killed them as they clutched one another.

My father wasn't the eldest but the first
who was born on this side and lived. Another
brother came between Abe and him (Abe cannot
even remember the name), and my father was cherished,
spoiled rotten. With such delusions of grandeur
how could he admit to his father's life
and work frivolity, garishness, the glitz
of circuses, and their brown animal smells?

5

And on their side? What they demanded of him
I dare not even imagine, attainments, perfections,
the fulfillment of dreams no flesh and blood child
could ever manage. That he did as well as he did
was a marvel, but it cost him. To be ignored
I sometimes think is a great gift, as my aunt,
a mere girl, was—who later could afford
to take a job distributing skin-flicks
in which the performers kept their hats on and wore
(the studios must have been chilly) socks—costumes.

6

My father never spoke about this either,
although his sister's irregular regular wages
helped get him and his younger brother through school
and kept a roof over their heads. My aunt,
who thought it was funny, was right. And later she married
my uncle who traveled for Jewish charities with
those same curious films in the trunk of his car
to get the sports into a giving mood.
My grandfather, had he not been dead by then,
might have enjoyed the joke. But not my father.

7

Whatever they wore here, however they spoke
or carried on, my grandfather would have thought them
outlandish, clowns he kept in stitches. A man
with his griefs—that baby, that homeland,
the world's pretense at making sense gone,
ripped like a basted seam, melted like shoddy
goods in a rainstorm . . . What did he care what they

thought (whoever *they* were)? A man with a load
of heavy stones cannot imagine men
who bear no such burdens, who float, *Luftmenschen*.

    8
On the other hand, drum rolls and the hushed attention
to those diminutive figures way up there
in grandpa's flashy suits, bathing in light,
who dared thin air and leapt to their conclusions
on another trapeze . . . that was serious stuff,
death-defying! Would the clothing, discarded,
be soaked in blood or just sweat? Is there
a difference? My father didn't think so. Exams
at school were trials, as, later, his trials in courtrooms
were exams, high-wire acts in the family circus.

    9
It is spring; the sap is rising; and the rubes
rise to their feet as we climb, rung by rung,
that awesome pole that holds the big top up
to the tiny platform. Down below, your father,
my son, stands watch as we whirl over his head
like gnats, like furies but tiny at that distance.
We would call down assurances of our loves,
but he can't hear us, fears for us, fears us,
as we let go, fly off, fly back, and hug,
holding onto each other, as if for dear life,

    10
but nowhere near so desperate or serious. Later,
from our dressing room, while getting out of our costumes,
we hear the drums and applause in antiphonal salvos
but give our attention to hangers that stir in the closet
like wind chimes in a garden. As if in a seance,
it could be grandpa signaling his approval,
or merely a greeting. I have his name; we have
his blood; you have my grandfatherly love—tepid,
comfortably vague, and yet reliable, like
an old socialist's dream of brotherhood.

Henry Taylor Shows Me His Parents' Barn

Beyond the condo's curtain wall, the Tetons
range, grand, wild, north to Grand
Teton and Teewinot—the brochures warn
of bears. I scan real estate ads, note
prices, imagine a life here, as all my life
I've done, on the Cape, in Miami, and other addresses
to which the rich and restless resort. I can't
afford more than to window-shop or to buy
a hat, boots, some souvenir to suggest
a recognizable past, but those hard faces
of gneisses and schists don't give. I'm not from here.
I think of the homelier hills in Loudoun County,
Virginia, where Henry Taylor showed me his parents'
barn less than a week ago. That country
is tame compared to this; even its shadows
must be familiar to one who grew up there; the patterns
of cloud crossing the sky are habitual; wind
that sings in the branches and brooks that purl in their gullies
are conformable to the ear as the songs one's mother
used to hum, unthinking. From the green
jumble on a boundary fence, he named
half a dozen vines, all childhood friends
of his and his father's, and farther back. The barn
was one of a very few in that county that dated
back before the war, and he told me how:
his great grandmother (I think it was)
took a chance—what was the risk if she failed?—
and had the barn emptied, all its provender
arrayed in the field he pointed to. The order
the Union detail had was to burn the barns
and the crops in the fields that Mosby's Raiders needed
to keep going. But the Taylor woman argued
with the sergeant or maybe second lieutenant that barns
were useless to Mosby; it was the *stuff* he wanted—
and there it all was. She waved her arm
in the gesture I saw her great grandson enact.
Reluctant perhaps to seem mean to a woman
or impressed by her wit, by the sheer nerve of it, he

gave in, gave the order. And the barn
stands there still, not as old as the hills
but older than most of the barns in Loudoun County.
My grandchildren, my children, my sister and I,
our mother and father, their mothers and fathers . . .
none of us could put down, filling out forms,
the same place of birth two generations
running. Running, hating to look back, we
do not have maps on the walls with names of distant
uncles and nearby streams keeping each other
alive in memory. I envy and honor
that close connection to land, and fear for it too.
Washington's urban sprawl and Baltimore's
threaten. Less forgiving than that lieutenant,
invulnerable to shame and pity, they will
smudge his county's known features strange,
to the blur I drive through, fly over, land on,
and skitter away from, having no hill of my own
no turn in the road, no color, smell, or light
like an old hat, conformed by usage to heads
I carry around in mine. I do not make
light of what it cost his people; it wasn't
easy, the barn standing empty, the yield
gone, like that, in a quarter hour's blaze.
It couldn't have been easy but it was
bearable—a small hardscrabble blessing.

Plodders

Consider the unclever. I
envy them rather. They do not try

but dimly rouse themselves to their half-
wakefulness. They never laugh,

say clever things, or write them. Stolid,
earnest, sober, very solid,

they go about their jobs and lives.
We are the ones who, sharp as knives,

have to worry lest we lose
our edges. They don't. Like old shoes,

they're comfy, good for years of service.
(We're unreliable and nervous.)

They are, on the whole, a happy crew.
I envy them. (I envy you.)

Lummox

As large as a water buffalo or larger,
but shaggy—there may be some woolly mammoth
in the bloodline—the lummox grazes the high plains.

Shy, easily spooked, they are homely beasts,
ungainly. . . . Hell, most people think, plain ugly.

Every so often it blinks its large eyes.
Now and then, it yawns.

Hard to imagine, but thousands of years ago
they roamed the continent in vast numbers,
thundering herds of lummoxen, a moving
ocean of flesh, now storming and now still.

Is it fanciful to suppose some dim
dream persists of that stamping ground
to haunt the rare relict that now and then
startles ranchers or backwoods campers?

Nearly tame now, and harmless,
its days of glory are gone, and we poke fun,
calling it clumsy and dumb.
It doesn't argue but only blinks, yawns,
then turns and ambles back into the woods.

Fizz

Not altogether pleasant, as we remember
from our first sip, those little bubbles bitter
but also lively on the tongue, the tickle
a tart treat, but here was wetter water
to slake the thought of thirst. More popular, pop
cuts the tang with sugar, but this betrays
the charge of the thing, that almost metallic play
on the nerves of the lolling tongue's sybaritic meat
by the Vichy Celestin, Apollinaris,
Perrier, or simply Good Health Seltzer
in cheap litre bottles, that fluttery fizz
that, if it were any sharper, would make us laugh
or gasp. Even the best still water, chilled
and served in crystal, cannot satisfy this
acquired taste. On a hot day, the gods
came down from Olympus for ambrosia
that hissed and sparkled hymns as this does.
                                                                                    So?
So . . . let that crystal goblet with still water
be married love in its normative (natural?)
condition; and let the other be the other:
those lively bubbles are secrets, and the pressure
is the self-consciousness errant spouses learn
not only for what's obvious, self-protection,
but out of consideration—tact demands it
and these are not unkindly people. The tart
truth that tingles so on the tongue burns,
hurts, but even for this one comes to acquire
a tolerance, even a taste, knowing full well
that if it were sharper, one would laugh or gasp.
Popular culture gets it wrong, puts sugar
into everything, but this alertness, charged,
has nothing to do with sweetness. Those who persist
discover what the gods on Olympus showed us
so often, coming down from their mountaintop
for the tonic of this ambrosia, this sparkle nothing
is quite like. This is that wetter water.

Sonnet

It needs to be renewed or, say, to have
its scab picked off to expose again the raw
wound; love needs its pain revivified.

When does a mother feel more intensely her
love for her child than in the night's dark hours
when the innocent infant burns with fever? Pity,
if it does not curdle, anneals, making love stronger.
Returning to a wife, what brute would not
adore her, pity her trust, and adore her more?

He feels the original ache, his ardor vivid
as in the beginning. Merely to stay home
is to dare dullness, to settle. But this more active
choice is refining, the instant's honesty,
even, perhaps, a kind of fidelity.

Rite for a Deceased Cat

We are all going to die—as all of us know,
that knowledge being the penalty we pay
for temporal lobes and the habit we've picked up
of looking ahead in time, as animals don't.

    ℣: Such unadorned statement of truth is not amusing.
    ℟: A regrettable and, one hopes, infrequent lapse.

They graze in grace those fields of here and now
that we have lost. Hawks and vultures hover
ever overhead in our clear air,
or are they motes that float in nervous eyes?

    ℣: One tries to avoid certain unpleasant subjects.
    ℟: Milk or lemon in your nose, Mr. Morgan?

Whether the fatty liver was cause or result
of the anorexia, experts could not say.
It seemed that the cat had retreated somewhere inward,
her appetites sated at last, even for being.

    ℣: I have, I fear, a subsequent engagement.
    ℟: There is only one way to skin a cat.

Her taste was for *nature morte*. The slightest movement
affronted her eye, but a quick claw could fix it
in a stillness which, in the end, she joined, herself.
Light as a shadow, she now is a shadow's shadow.

    ℣: A shadow in darkness. I shudder to think.
    ℟: Precisely.

Or, better, recall that watchful motionlessness
with which she stalked a mole or squirrel or unwary
bird. Imagine completion and perfection
of that breathless poise: she does not need to pounce.

    ℣: As my own pulse slows, the moment expands.
    ℟: My eyelids narrow; my horizon widens.

Like an abandoned vessel, the body's bulk
wallows in heavier weather, loses way.
It takes a long time before she goes down.
We're moved but then lose interest and even patience.

℣: Nevermind. It doesn't matter much.
℟: I couldn't have put it any better, myself.

Still, we miss her, admittedly less each day
as the expectation of her nimble lighting
on the foot of the bed diminishes. Heartlessness,
the hard lesson she teaches, we learn at last.

℣: Fastidiousness and the grace to see what is.
℟: Pray for us at the hour of our death.

Flea

With practice, you learn their likely trails and how
to nab them as they scurry into the deeper
forests of thicker hair. It takes patience and quickness,
but the reward—the sweet pop of their bodies' crack
on the flat of your fingernail—is huge, out of all
proportion to their size or the occasion.
Your dog lies supine, his lips falling
upward into a goofy grin. Your lips
are pursed in concentration as you hunt
among those specks of dried blood they leave behind—
their spoor is camouflage—a moving speck.

They seem shrewd, endowed with a clever set
of genetic preferences for those likely places—
beneath the tail, in the ears, or inside the thighs—
wherever they can feed and not be worried
by dog teeth. The human nail is hardly
an ideal instrument. Not every grab succeeds,
and even when you've managed to catch one, it wriggles
in your fat fingertip's pillow, its carapace
all but indestructible. You pill roll, try
to maneuver it onto the flat of the nail, and then,
with a nail of the other hand, steam-roller it dead.

Misery, misery, misery, misery . . .
that's what it is, and that's what you've obliterated,
at least for the moment, at least this tiny speck
of parisitism, of filth, of evil . . . What else
is there in this life, beyond The Pursuit
of the Good and The Struggle with Evil? That insignificant
bloody speck is the seed of the plagues of Europe,
or more modestly but more pressingly all
the imperfections of that paragon life a poodle
ought to lead. Not even his cushion is safe,
but has to be sprayed or powdered, laundered and poisoned.

This maculate blood left on the fingernails
is fascinating, a sign—but of what? In what
do we still believe? Blood sacrifice

is a bit *vieux jeux*; one hardly dares admit
how killing is fun, making us mere men
feel for an instant greater, even the equals
of gods, which is why we share the moment and part
of the prize as well with those haughty beings. I offer
this kill of mine to any god willing
to explain himself, or even own to a world
in which fleas forage on the belly of an old dog.

Satisfaction

News has come today that one
I hate and whom my parents hated
is stricken. His days are nearly done.
Would that they'd waited

to hear these tidings and to share,
as I think they might have, my reaction
which isn't pleasure so much as a bare-
boned satisfaction.

I like to think of how their prayers
and curses have at last an answer.
Patience is all in these affairs.
That he has cancer

and that all those nice metastases
are blooming like flowers everywhere
is charming news but it would please
me more to hear

that his disease will run a course
both slow and painful—for my trust is
not in mercy but the force
of simple justice:

Let him writhe all night and feel
a taste on this earth of the pain
he's earned. If Dante's hell were real
and it could rain

molten lead down on his head
and I could see it and my father
with me . . . But he'll soon be dead.
Why should I bother

dreaming up elaborate
torments? What the world has served
up for him on his china plate
is well deserved

and will suffice. And when I rise
early to peer at songbirds flying
across the light, I'll rub my eyes . . .
and think, he's dying.

Snowfall

The glee of children at the season's first
snow fuzzes over, quick as a branch
the flakes have piled on. We can remember something
of what we felt years ago, but the spirit
no longer leaps up. Now we take care
where we put our feet. We watch the amazing
streaming of the snow in the glare of street lamps,
but think what it will cost to have it shoveled.
Worse, I see what the young children don't:
in a field, tracks of hunger stalking terror
to red flecks in the snow; or beyond, another
larger field where nothing at all has touched
that terrible white plane. Laughter rings
in the air as I look down, watching my step.

Letter to a Grandchild

Sir or Madame . . . I cannot address you better,
being unaware as I set down this letter
what sex you are. And Occupant won't do.
I dare say that you've grown accustomed to
those comfy digs you're in; your new address
will be a coming down, I fear—a mess
you won't get used to, not even someday
(I haven't, yet). Therefore in any way
to refer even obliquely to such a tender
subject would be unfeeling, a tactless blunder.
I know, of course you didn't volunteer
to be born. Who would? It just happens, my dear,
and you'll look up and blink at us while we
congratulate the parents and look to see
how tiny the baby fingernails are, how bright
the eyes, and offer thanks that it's all right
with mother and infant. Nobody condoles
with the new being for this change in roles
from generality to private person, toy
of the fates like all the rest of us, girl or boy.
Well, I shan't either, or not explicitly, though
you'll learn how to see through *praeteritio*
quickly enough with parents like yours. They're not
so bad as you'll think one day, or quite so hot
as I think they are now. So far you've been
lucky I think, but hold that toothless grin.
How far will that luck take you? Can it hold
forever? You will grow up and grow old,
learning the bitter truths that everyone learns—
what's hard, what's sharp, what freezes, and what burns
inside and goes on hurting. It would be sappy
to ignore all that and just hope that you're happy
for ever and ever. Happiness, said Flaubert,
is easy if you're stupid and selfish—there
is also health you need, but that's the whole
trick. The simple sybaritic goal
won't do for one who's yet to compromise,
flatter, cajole, say mean things, or tell lies . . .

I wish you better and richer. I wish you grace
of body and spirit, that you may make the place
you're in a little more splendid—as you will
in your first moments with us, and may still
as you learn to creep and babble. Keep that up.
Smile and chortle as you fling your cup
from the high chair tray. You'll quickly figure out
your own style—of that I have no doubt.
I wish you, too, the strength you'll need to endure
whatever your intelligence or your
generous spirit is drawn to, that you may find
some way to bear the things most of us blind
ourselves to and ignore. Be useful, cheerful,
and patient. Yes, I know, that's quite an earful
I'm offering you. And your ear is very small.
But I shall write this out, to hang on the wall
where it will look down upon you until rather
later when you may read what your grandfather
wishes for you and of you. I'll close with this
not least significant of promises—
that we be careful with each other, and try
tact and forbearance, for you are my future and I
am your past, which is a peculiar kind of relation
imposing a difficult mutual obligation
to excellence, that we each contrive to live
as well as we can, and also to forgive
the other's demand to do just a little better—
which is never wholly welcome. I end this letter
with sincere best wishes. Is that perhaps too chilly?
Formal, rather. One ought not be silly
especially on great occasions such
as this. But relax. We shall stay in touch,
exchanging presence and presents as is done
with grandparent and granddaughter or grandson
who celebrate and amuse each other maybe,
their hopes thus born or freshened. Blessings, baby!

Another Letter to a Grandchild

Listen, kid, you've had it all your way
long enough now. A dog may have his day
but not ten months. You've run your mom and dad
ragged, haggard. I love you, but I'm sad
to see you tyrannizing others I love
also. You've developed this trick of
waking up at two and three and four
in the morning to howl for attention. It's a bore
they'll train you out of sooner or later (I vote
for sooner). Oh, they gaze at you and dote
but their eyes have circles under them—not nice.
I think of your father holding that piece of ice
to his split lip where you butted him for fun,
or of his younger brother—my other son—
and the angry welt on his shoulder where you'd bit
him with those razor-sharp teeth. What is this shit?
The literal kind we take from you is quite
sufficient, thank you. You'll learn to sleep all night
or they'll wring your little neck, or maybe I
will do it for them. Oh, yes, you're quite a guy,
but somewhat spoiled. You must not be misled
by these indulgent people, or take to head
and heart their excessive forbearance, or depend
too much upon it. I watch as you extend
your arm in a bye-bye wave, a fascist salute
we all return (which even you think is cute).
You disappear up the stairway, waving. That's a
clever boy! (But this is no Piazza
Venezia, kiddo!) I tell your parents how
they ought to put their feet down with you now,
and let you cry—for hours, all night long
if it comes to that. You're learning a lot of wrong
things if you think you can simply yell and be
amused, dandled, cuddled, sung to. We
didn't like it either, but we have all
experienced that pain of Adam's fall
from some perfection none of us can quite
remember. When you wake up in the night

you can survive, silent, alone, as we
have had to learn ourselves, and patiently,
suppressing those enraged or anguished howls.
It's a lot to ask. As is control of the bowels
and bladder. Civilization's discontents
(I'll send you the book one day) make perfect sense
when you reflect on the alternative:
barbarity and its gratifications. Live
your life like that and you'll learn well enough
what loneliness is like. I know, it's tough,
but look how you've come along, nudging us higher
up on the family tree. We did not aspire
to those loftier, frailer boughs, and yet we will
give way to you, and gracefully, though chill
winds may shake us. We don't cry out, either,
but do what we can to shield you from the weather.
When the bough breaks, your cradle will not fall,
but one of us. That heartbeat in your small
chest, your delicate pulse, your effortless breath
are monstrous harbingers. We can forgive you death
and cuddle you close as you clutch some stuffed toy,
and sing to you, and call you a clever boy. . . .
In exchange for this, we give you small demands
for you to rattle in your pudgy hands,
put in your mouth and try to chew on, perhaps
fling away. Are there any more in our laps?
Or maybe they will all simply disappear—
You wonder whether we'll bring them back? My dear,
again and again, until you recognize
that even kings have councils to advise
them what they can and can't do. No one's free,
and no one's id, imperious, can be
that dictator you'd like us all to obey.
You remind us, though, of how it was that day
we bumped our own delicate heads on the same
hard truth. It is, indeed, a crying shame,
your mother, father, and I agree. But they
can't take any more. You'll have to learn to play
alone in your crib or with those animals
you sleep with every night, all your plush pals.

The rest will follow, as surely as the sun
rises in the east, which is how that's done
every morning. Darkness is nothing to fear—
or nothing for someone like you, not even a year
old, to worry about. For us, it's another
story, which one day your father or mother
may explain. But don't fret. That will keep.
Till then, you be a good baby. And sleep.

Solstice

A ghost of a sun flees from the sky as I,
the son of a ghostly father, hurry—to keep
blood circulating in the cold—to buy
another Yahrzeit candle in its cheap
glass I'll use for juice. I don't believe
in any of this, but he did, and I'd rather
feel like a fool than a bum. To think, to grieve,
to remember isn't enough. One must go to the bother
of doing something. Parents and children trade
places after awhile. I learned to endure
the whims, and accommodate to demands he made,
as he had done for mine once. Fewer and fewer
remain except for this minimal annual task.
A postcard comes from the people who did the stone
that marks the grave, so I don't have to ask
what date the Hebrew lunacy falls on.
They put it to me: will I refuse to do
what I know he would have wanted? I give in,
go out, come back again, still wanting to
earn praise as the good boy I've never been.
And when the sun has given up, I give
lip service, mumble the prayer, and light the wick.
It's guaranteed that the little flame will live
the whole twenty-four hours, which seems a trick
for two and three-quarter ounces of parafin.
All night shadows will dance on the ceiling and play
on the walls. And as I pass, I will glance in
to see how it's doing during the next day.
The flame is life, but the candle's guttering is
a reenacting of the death. I take
small satisfaction in my bearing this
as well as I do. I know it's for my sake
as much as his that I do this. My eyes brim,
but that can happen at the movies. Say
rather that I've bargained once more with him
and done what he wanted, only to keep him at bay.

Equinox

Ten Broken Stanzas for my Sister

1

A balance shifts, and we can feel the night
heavy in the scale; darkness and cold
will weigh with us from now on. In decline
the sun will make its doddering round of days
that are less than days, the ghosts of days; the weather
will turn; and the year, stricken, will sicken unto
death.
      It is all just as it ought to be.
This is the day when we call one another
to exchange whatever comfort we can. This is
the day mother was murdered. And the sun
ought to blanch, to blench in shame. For all
our days are ghosts. This is our time of year.

2

In Yiddish, *Yahrzeit*. There is no English word
that serves correctly. Anniversary
is gay, wears party hats, has dinner out,
but *Yahrzeit* tells the time by throbs of pain,
mourns the turning of each season's screws,
and can predict by inner aches the outer
weather,
      as the wounded learn to do
from predictable cycles of agony and numbness.
Pain and its diminution are the two
companions we trust, stars in our firmament.
We also have the telephone and each other.

3

The world being what it is, it has a term
describing us. The social scientists call
us "catastrophic orphans," and study us
along with survivors of floods and such disasters,
and also torture victims. One theory holds
that the chemistry of the brain undergoes some change

so that everything else changes
                              for them, for us.
It's plausible perhaps. At least we know
that what we know, we know. The others are lucky
and, whatever their ages, innocent as children.
We talk sometimes as children, but hurt children.

    4

One would suppose the past to be secure,
but no, its memories, even locked away,
are vulnerable to any passing thug
or crazy who can crawl through a cellar window
to wreak his retroactive havoc on any
treasure he fouls. The house, and the sense we had
of place that an alewife has or a spawning salmon
can find in its right river and freshwater pond
of welcome and safety is lost,
                              burgled, robbed.
Sickened, we swim through indifferent seas, all
salty, none worth notice. I would not,
hating that place, go back even to die.

    5

Whatever people live for, happy times,
the milestones of graduations, weddings, births,
occasions of reunion and rejoicing,
these are tainted. Now, no good news comes
but with its confirming pang
                              that she has not
heard it, shared it, lived to see what she
would have blessed. And that lack of her blessing is
accursed. No child of ours achieves, enjoys
good fortune but to start our scalding tears.
Dutiful children, we rub our eyes with our fists
as she would have us do, we are sure, having
learned from her what good manners demand.

    6

It doesn't get better. Years have gone by
and the only change is that we no longer expect
or fear that we may somehow regain our old

lives and selves. We are like the religious
brothers and sisters of some strict observance,
except that we do not pray, unless to bear
witness is a kind of prayer.
                            I doubt it.
What kind of play is it when Orestes
only shakes his head when Electra calls
to complain or, worse, not to complain but like
a good sister cheer him a little, to help him
bear it, bear up, get through another week?
    7
The earth itself is the great mother, Gaea.
The Judeo-Christian view, always upward,
ignores such perceptions, primitive, basic,
as are under their very noses. The ground we walk
no longer springs, for the converse is also true,
that Mother was the earth. Her murder pollutes
like a chemical seepage or oil spill, and the fish
die and the birds and animals drop. On the news,
the clips are horrible, horrible.
                            You and I,
stricken, can take grim satisfaction in these
dreadful confirmations that our worst
truth is not the exception, but that our
suffering has its company, is the rule.
    8
We keep a few relics. I take care
of a pot of her African violets. Still alive,
they bloom in the spring and make me weep. But we,
being parts of her, are each other's keepsakes,
what's best of what is left of her, which changes
all the rules, for we must be good children,
tender with one another as if she had only
left the room a moment and would be back
to call us to account.
                        She is not watching
which puts us on our honor. What's hard to learn
is to forgive each other, as she would have done,
and harder, hardest, to forgive ourselves.

9
All day I have been playing Pergolesi's
Stabat Mater, the melancholy of it
bearably remote: dog-Latin, Catholic.
And yet, the two voices, the boy soprano
and countertenor, are close enough,
                                        ours,
echoing, harmonizing and descanting,
as we do. "*Eja, Mater, fons amoris* . . ."
and I can scarcely breathe, for the gentleness
that cradled us from a brute and ugly world
is gone, and we are bereft. But like those two,
in harmony. A solo voice would be
intolerable. At least we are together.

10
The other blessing is that the cold will come.
The season is turning, has turned, and the first
frost will come with its usual relief,
killing by hundreds of millions flies, mosquitoes,
midges, and other such creatures that teemed and annoyed
for what seemed at the time a long time. The stars
will twinkle again in icy-clear air with a hint
of anaesthesia if not peace, those scary
spaces in between impressive . . .
                                        We don't
believe in souls up there spinning around
forever like Laika but emptiness, cold
and darkness are good enough. I'd call that heaven.